MW00800305

wered in the cerebrum. Thus by prayer to God
hin, and in no other way, can man overcome the ad-
sary or the "carnal mind which is at enmity to God."
All so-called sex reform that tolerates union of sexes,
y be answered by:
There is a way that
Seemeth right to man,
The end of which is death."
In my Kingdom there is no marrying nor giving in marriage,
But they are as the
Angels in Heaven."
No page of the wonders of the human body—the tem-
: of the living God—is more divinely scientific than the
rable that follows:
'The foolish man built his house on the sand
And the rain washed it away."
'The wise man built his house on a rock
And it stood the storms, for it was builded upon a rock."
The Bible is a compilation of astronomical, physiolog-
l and anatomical symbols, allegories and parables.
In the technical terms of modern chemistry and physi-
gy the above text is explained as follows: Sand and
nent form rock or stone. Sand alone, without some
dium—cement—is unstable, simply "shifting sand."
The Pineal gland, the *dynamo* that runs the organism
man, is composed of sand plus a cement, an ointment,
mear, found, as has been explained, in the spinal cord,
o to some extent, in all parts of the body. When this
nent is wasted, as the Prodigal Son wasted his sub-
nce in riotous living, there being a deficiency of this
ecious oil, the pineal gland becomes pasty, and does
t vibrate at a rate that vitalizes the blood and tissue at
e health and strength rate, and the house, beth or body,
ls.
In the common slang of the hour, we say: "He lacks
e sand," or "grit."
The mineral salts of blood were called sand or salt by
e Greeks. The cell-salts that are found in the pineal
and are chiefly potassium phosphate, the base of the
ay matter of the brain, and lime, but all of the 12 inor-
nic salts are represented. In Revelation, the pineal

gland is called "the white stone." In Biochemistry, the phosphate of potassium is given as the birth salt of Aries people.

Those who build their house upon a rock are they who conserve the substance that unites with the sand—cell-salts—and thus form the rock upon which a body may be built that will be free from sin and sickness.

The mission of Jesus, the Christ, was to *triumph over death* and the grave, over matter, and transmute his body and also materialize at will. He not only succeeded in doing this, but stated most emphatically that all the things that he did, we may do also.

Did he proclaim the truth?

Answer, thou of little faith!

> "Rock of Ages, cleft for me,
> Let me hide myself in thee."

NOAH, THE ARK AND THE ANIMALS

FEW theologians are there, of to-day, who insist on a literal interpretation of the biblical story of the flood, Noah and the ark.

There are known to be 1656 species of mammals; 6266 species of birds; 642 of reptiles; 20 of oxen; 27 species of goats; 48 species of antelopes; insects, fish, turtles and creeping things on land and sea innumerable.

There is not a bit of geological evidence that the earth was ever totally submerged. But, going to the root of the words Noah, ark, Ararat, etc., it is quite easy to read the riddle of the allegory.

Noah is Hebrew for rest. Ararat simply means a mount or elevation. In English we say hill, mound, peak, mountain, etc. So in both Greek and Hebrew we find Nebo, Pisgah, Ararat, pinnacle of the temple, Zion, Gibeon, used to typify brain and pineal gland.

Ark, or boat, is used to symbol the seed (fish or Moses) born in the solar-plexus to be carried up through the regenerative process to the pineal gland. Moses was found in an ark and the ark of the covenant was carried by the children of Israel (see Jacob's 13 children) through the wilderness and *across* Jordan, where the "waters stood up at the City of Adam."

Adam means earth or sand. At the source of the spinal cord there is a body called medulla oblongata. Medulla means marrow or thick oil or ointment. This oblong body (oblongata in Latin) is a bed of mineral salts of the body and marrow. This precious oil (Christ) is received there by secretions from the cerebrum, the upper brain—the "Most High."

This oil flows down the spinal cord to the Caudia Equina, and this is a symbol of the Jordan and Dead Sea of Palestine.

Jordan means the "Descender" or oil flowing down. Witness: *Dove* or dive—to descend. Dove, *i. e.*, a diver

—"The Spirit of God descended like a dove, and a voice said, 'This is my Son,' " etc.

This occurred *after* the baptism of Jesus, the seed, in Jordan, the oil or Christ.

The animals taken up to Ararat, the pineal gland, or "Pinnacle of the temple," simply means the transmutation of animal desires and propensities by saving the ark (seed) and crucifying it at Golgotha where it *Crosses* Jordan in medulla, the "Place of the Skull."

Woman the 4th Dimension.

The solar system has entered the "Sign of the Son of Man," where it will remain for over 2000 years. In astrology this sign is symboled as "The Water Bearer," while in Bible Alchemy it is represented by Dan, the fifth son of Jacob, and means "judgment," or "he that judges."

From these statements it is easy to realize that all that is taking place in the world to-day is but a "working out" or a summing up of all that has been taking place for centuries.

The world is awakening, the old order is passing, worn-out traditions that are no longer applicable to present conditions must be replaced by new.

Radical and fundamental changes stare us in the face on all sides. Science, philosophy, religion, bodies politic and social—*all* are being shaken from their very foundations—to be rebuilt anew.

There is no equilibrium, no balance, no harmony, no equality, anywhere.

Nowhere do we see a better illustration of this unbalanced condition of the world than in man's attitude toward woman. For some time, now, this viewpoint has been gradually changing and Aquarian vibrations, or, in other words, the vibratory influence of the planets, have made conditions possible for this change.

Woman is at last coming into her own.

Co-equal with man! Mighty strides toward the regeneration of the human race will now be made.

With equilibrium of forces now possible world harmony shall grow apace.

All these truths can be mathematically expressed.

Four (4) means realization—one and three (1 plus 3) equals four.

Woman or mother comes from the Hebrew word Mem-M (womb, man, water, Mary—same meaning in all).

"I saw a woman clothed with the *Son*, the moon (from month-menses) under her *feet*. She controlled the twelve functions of the body. The Son signifies "Sun" or "Son of Man," the seed or product of her own life, saved and lifted up. The Moon refers to the generative life. Twelve stars are the twelve functions, typified by the twelve zodiacal signs which she has mastered through physical regeneration.

Having been upon the cross, or having crossed over, the seed is Christed, and in the man or woman seeking to regenerate or "save," the seed is *saved*, it then enters the Optic Thalamus, the eye of the chamber, which "giveth light to all that are in the house," that is, to the twelve functions that are in the body, represented by the twelve signs of the zodiac.

Woman regenerated—"clothed with the Sun"—is the Queen of Sheba, in Bible symbology, and is represented by the number seven (7).

Then woman is Queen of 7. Sheba is seven in Hebrew, and Solomon's temple (soul-of-man) is the physical body where the Queen of Sheba found so many wonders.

Queen of seven *what?*

Man is only three (3) dimensions.

Dimension means *line*.

The human body as well as the universe are geometrical figures, a fact which the old philosophers well knew, for they said that sound and number governed the laws of creation.

Man is proved to be a three dimensional creature by physiology; and woman is the fourth dimension, by the same means of proof.

In the thirty-first chapter of Jeremiah, twenty-second verse, we read: "A woman shall compass a man."

Mathematically, a woman can encompass a man.

Man cannot compass a woman, for he is only a three-line creature, while she is four. Therefore, four is able to compass, or contain within its radius, three.

Woman may be represented by the square (four lines).

Man may be represented by the triangle (three lines).

Three and four do not balance, and never have. There has not been universal harmony or balance between them, for man has never considered woman his equal until very recently.

But man is "coming off his high horse," and the scales will soon balance.

All down the ages man has considered himself the "lord of all creation." The "spare rib" which he so condescendingly parted with in the so-called "beginning" unbalanced him entirely. He considered himself superior to woman and has continued to do so to the "end of the world," or "whorl of activity"—the activity or manifestation of the solar system in the last or previous sign, that representing the water age.

During the water age man conquered the water—inventions pertaining to water were perfected, etc., etc.

To return to the mathematical equation of man and woman:

The three dimensions or lines of man that can be shown on a physiological chart are the creative centers of the brain, the solar plexus and the sex organs . Woman also possesses the creative centers of brain, solar plexus and sex organs; *but* she also possesses another, and in a way the most wonderful of all—the *breast* that nourishes infant man. This is the fourth dimension or line. These imaginary lines are at equal distances from each other.

Work this out for yourselves on the chart and you will never forget it.

In the triangle drawn to represent man we find the eye, also. This is a well-known Masonic symbol.

See "The *Rib-lah* that made the *Wom(b)an.*"

TRANSLATIONS OF SCRIPTURE.

"He that saveth his life shall lose it."—Mark 8:35.

THE above sentence does not ring true and is not logical.

A Greek professor recently went to Oxford, England, for the sole purpose of looking into the Greek text in regard to this seeming inconsistency. (Also Luke 16:9. See below.)

The discovery was made that the letter N (from nun, meaning a fish), was omitted, also the letter O, and that a correct translation reads: "He that saveth his life shall *loosen* it," etc.

The seed, in the fable, or Jesus, said: "I am the way, the truth and the *life*," etc. Therefore, he that saveth his life (Seed) shall loosen it so that it may enter the 'Strait and narrow way," etc. This strait is the Spinal Cord. As has already been written, "I am the bread of life." Again, "Cast thy bread upon the waters"—*i. e.,* the strait. Cast thy bread upon the water exactly harmonizes with "Loosen it."

Luke 16:9: "And I say unto you, make unto yourselves friends of the mammon of unrighteousness; that when ye fail they may receive you into everlasting habitations."

Literally the statement would nullify all the teaching of Jesus, and it is simply amazing that the so-called Christian world has so largely ignored it. However, a few critics from the orthodox ranks, not being at all satisfied with the rendering, have tried, in various ways, to reconcile the paradox, and to that end several pamphlets may be found in the theological departments of our colleges and universities.

Here is the explanation by a Greek scholar:

"Make unto your self *other* friends than those who worship the mammon of unrighteousness," etc.

[147]

Accepting the New Testament error, without questi[] accounts for the great anxiety shown by churches of [] denominations to secure the financial support of t[] wealthy, whether they be vital Christians, in belief, [] nominally so. Proof of which may be seen in the end [] the world, or age, nominally dominated by so-call[] Christianity.

Many worshipers of the mammon of unrighteousne[] exhibited much more horror over the destruction of cost[] cathedrals by the Huns than they did at the rape [] women and slaughter of children by the Germans in B[] gium, or murders by the sinking of the Lusitania.

Nothing can survive this "Day of Judgment" except [] be founded upon the Truth, which liveth and reigne[] forevermore.

JOSHUA COMMANDS THE SUN AND MOON TO STAND STILL

IN Physiological Chart the solar plexus, a round body of tissue ganglion, may be plainly seen. Attached to the SUN (center) is a body called semi-lunar ganglion (half moon), which is attached to the vertebra and spinal cord. A median line (across the center of body) will divide these organs, half above the line, half below.

The upper halves of the sun and moon vibrate for spiritual man and the lower half for *natural,* or animal man.

"There is a natural and a spiritual body."—Paul.

Now Joshua, the seed, on its way to the pineal gland is made to say, "Sun, stand thou still on Gibeon."

Gibeon means a mound or elevation. So the seed (Joshua, a fish), commands the animal vibration of *solar* (sun) plexus to stand still, *i. e.,* cease to continue to dominate the spiritual forces, "while I slay my enemies"— that is, the animal blood that predominates in carnal thought.

"And thou moon in the valley of Ajalon."

Ajalon means a "valley in Bethlehem," says a Bible dictionary.

Bethlehem—the house of bread: the *seed* is the bread.

Whoever conquers sex desire commands the sun and moon to stand still.

Who can do this?

"With man it is impossible, but with God all things are possible." Matt. 19th chapter.

Therefore, all can succeed by asking help from the "Most High."

A cloud of witnesses may be found to substantiate the statement made above that the sun and moon in the Joshua story refer to the solar plexus and semi-lunar ganglion.

Eph. in Hebrew is prefix to many words meaning the

centre or middle. It is defined in Smith's Bible Dictionary under the name Eph-ah, as "First in order of the sons of Midian, *i. e.,* strife or contention between Michael and Apollyon occurs in the center of the body where the animal continually fights the upper force that seeks to lift up and regenerate the animal or natural man.

Ephah also means weight (measure or balance, Libra, the scales).

Again, E-phes-dammin, "boundary of animal blood."

"I fought with wild beasts at Ephesus."—Paul.

Ephesians are the children of Ephesus, the solar plexus, therefore the seed. Paul the still small voice, or intuition, redeeming (lifting up).

The seeds constitute Paul's Epistle to the Ephesians.

Once more: "Eph-raim is joined to his idols; let him alone."

This epigram defines the physical man, "Dead in trespass and sin"—one who cannot be awakened by reasoning with him.

GLOSSARY

The Meaning of Glory

GLORY is derived from glow and ray—to illumine, to light.

Prof. Smiley, formerly teacher of Greek in Cornell University, writes: "The body is a lamp and this oil (referring to the oil descending the spinal cord) is its illuminating fluid."

Prof. Smiley also says: "This oil, in Greek, is from the root letters X. P. I.—Chrism or Chri"—Greek for oil, or Christ. "The *Christ in you*, the hope (substance) of glory," or light.—Paul.

But, says Paul, "If ye have only *hoped* Christ, ye are of all men most miserable." Why?

For "Unless Christ be *raised* our preaching is vain." The *only* way to *raise* THIS oil is by the seed entering the spinal cord and lifting up the oil. "If I (Jesus, the seed) be lifted up, I will draw *all* men (se-men, or oil) unto me."

Thus is the command, "Give one-tenth (tithe) unto the Lord," obeyed.

"The *entrance* of *thy word* giveth light"; "The seed is the WORD."—Luke.

John, Johannes, or Ioannes, means OIL, also an ointment, and "Came to bear witness of that *light*." St. John 1:6.

Again—"That the Father may be glorified in the Son." John 14:13.

"Father, the hour has come; glorify thy Son, that thy Son may glorify thee."

Lip service cannot glow-ray or glorify God, but the seed "which is Christ" (Paul), saved and lifted up, carries illuminating oil to the Father, enters the optic in the thalamus and giveth light. "And the temple needs no other light."

We feel sure that those who desire the whole truth in regard to the real meaning of "glory" and "glorify"

will esteem it their duty and privilege to read St. Jo
and especially verses 22 and 24 of the 17th Chap
also 19th verse of the 21st Chapter.

The word Saint means a perfect person, or one v
realizes that Perfection even as the Father is perf
According to the teachings of Scripture, the *Only* v
that perfection can be attained is by saving the seed a
thus be "Born of God."

The ancient painters painted a halo or a "nimbus
gold-colored light," as Walt Whitman sang, about
head of the Madonna, the infant Jesus and many of
saints and prophets. Hence we infer that the idea of
illuminating oil prevailed all down the ages.

The Greek epic of the vestal Virgins keeping the
or light forever burning and the wise virgins with lar
filled with oil, bear witness to the cosmic belief that th
is a *substance* in man that enlightens and redeems, if
destroyed by animal forces.

OUR EVER-PRESENT HELP

"For who maketh thee to differ from another? A
what hast thou that thou *didst not receive?* Now if t
didst receive it, why dost thou glory, as if thou ha
not received it?"

"What! Know ye not that your body is the tem
of the Holy Ghost which is *in you*, which ye have of G
and ye are not your own?"

"For ye are *bought with a price*," etc. See "Give o
tenth to the Lord," etc.

"Is not my help *in me?* And is wisdom driven qu
from me?" Job 6:13.

"Send the help from the *sanctuary*, and strength
thee *out of* Zion." (See explanation of these terms
glossary.)

"Our soul waiteth for the Lord; he is our help a
our shield."

"God is our refuge and strength, a *very present* h
in trouble."

"I will lift up mine eyes unto the hills, or mountai
from whence cometh my help." "Mount of the Lor
the upper brain, "Most High."

THE TEMPLE OF GOD

"Know ye not that ye are the temple of God and that the spirit of God dwelleth in you? If any man defile the temple of God, him shall God destroy; for the temple of God is holy, which temple ye are." Man defiles the temple by preventing the seed (the *word*) from going up, or returning to the upper brain, the cerebrum. In short, he eats of the fruit of the tree of life, and therefore it cannot arise or return to the Kingdom, the optic thalamus, and become the "Light in the chamber," where it may "Cleanse from all sin."

He that overcometh (does not eat or destroy the seed, allows it "to remain in him") "I will give to eat of the tree of life in the *"Father's Kingdom."* See Lord's Supper.

The tree of life is the Vagus nerve (pneumogastric) and its branches. (See article on Vagus nerve.)

Whose branches, or nerves, are called Nazareth, which is Greek for shoot, sprout or twigs—little branches; hence, "Jesus of Nazareth, whom thou persecuteth."

Jesus, the seed, thus speaks to Saul, who, after conversion, no longer used "S" (Schin or sin), but substituted "P," speech or "going forth, radiating," and thus became Paul the preacher.

Paul means "small" and refers to the seed itself. After the crucifixion of Jesus (the seed), the parable makes another seed take the place of the first-born, and thus says, "I was born out of time."

SAUL OF TARSUS

Tarsus means "foot." Pisces, the fishes, are represented by the feet. In regard to "small," read the parable of the "mustard seed."

"IN MY KINGDOM"

"He that is born in thy house shall not be thine heir, but he that cometh forth out of *thine own bowels* shall be thine heir."

"She that is desolate hath many more children than she that hath an husband."

Here is proof that in the regeneration, that is, the plan of salvation *above* the solar plexus, there is no marrying nor *giving* in marriage, for male and female are the same. Both have the same manger or WOMB, in man, both the same Ida and Pingala, or Joseph and Mary; and the same pneumogastric nerve that brings down the same Holy Ghost—breath—that conceives the seed, Jesus. Hence, Peter reads thus: "Born not of corruptible seed but of incorruptible; the Word of God."

So, then, male and female in the new order MUST WORK OUT THEIR OWN SALVATION, the saving seed that is in each separate body.

No sex reform, no physical contact—"Thou shalt not touch it"—Genesis; no effort to "climb up some other way" is tolerated, in the GREAT TEXT BOOK OF PHYSIOLOGY, THE HOLY BIBLE, or *whole book*.

THE BELOVED CATHOLIC PRIEST

Father John A. Ryan lays it down as "a fundamental ethical principle" that sexual intercourse for any other object than procreation is unnatural and "a perversion of the generative faculty on exactly the same moral level as the practice of the solitary vice."

"THE TREE OF LIFE"

The branches of the Vagus, or pneumogastric nerve, which extend to lungs and stomach, are called the "Tree of Life."

The oil or substance that flows down the plexus of nerves that branch off from the main nerve is deposited in the manger (the nun) or mouth of the fish, and forms a seed or *fruit* of the tree. This seed, being formed of the Esse of God, is called the Son of God, also the Son of Man that has "Power *in* earth (the body) to forgive sins. This seed says, "I am the way, the truth and the life"—hence the "Tree of Life."

THE ONLY CAUSE OF OLD AGE

Youth, strength and health depend entirely upon the automatic action of the blood which deposits the material (itself) formed from the Esse, or substance called air, the breath of God, and the residue (ashes) of food, the mineral salts, and deposits it in the upper chamber, the cerebrum (Most High), the hallowed or hollowed place. (See fatted calf or Kaph.)

The secretions descending from this fat, oil the place of the secretions, build and sustain the entire bodily structure. But, if a certain amount, "one-tenth," is not returned, the reservoir becomes depleted day by day until the deficiency, or sin (*i.e.*, falling short) causes weakness, decrepitude, etc., which we, in our ignorance, have called "old age."

The Bible tells the cause and the remedy, thus: "The wages of sin is *death.*"

But, "His delight is in the law of the Lord," *then*: He shall be like a tree planted by the river of waters that bringeth forth its fruit in its season; but his leaf also shall *not wither*, and whatsoever he doeth shall *prosper.*"

There is one cause of old age and one only: wasting the LIFE FORCE, the gray matter of the brain, the SEED, the WORD of God, which, if *saved*, results in THE WORD MADE FLESH."

When people say unto you, "Lo! here," or "Lo! there is the cause of old age," believe them not, for the cause of old age is within YOU.

SAMSON OR SAM SUN

The letter S in Hebrew is the 15th of the alphabet, and symbolizes the great dragon, the Great Dragon of the Threshold. In Hebrew it is Samech. The stomach is also symbolical of this letter. Here, also, is the Solar Plexus, the Sun Center or Son. Likewise, the physical power of the mind is centered here, the desire for Animal vibration, the "things thy soul lusteth after."

Samson, in Smith's Bible Dictionary, also means "Sun-like, strong, distinguished."

Gaza simply means the "strong," or "strong city."

Delilah means "weak, feeble," or "to pine with desire," and the symbolism is wrought into the form of a woman that tempted Samson, to destroy his strength by yielding to desire, or Delilah.

After sufficient time had elapsed in which material for a new seed could descend (as in the case of Hiram Abiff, in Freemasonry), Samson, through prayer, was able to save the seed, and was then spiritually strong, thus giving him strength to tear down the Strong City of Gaza, or "Carry away the pillars of Gaza."

The reader is urged to study carefully the 13th Chapter of Judges to the 16th.

The story of the birth of Jesus and the warnings and prophecies concerning Samson are almost identical. He is even called "A Nazarite," which means, in Hebrew, "One consecrated to God."

In the story of Samson we read how he went down to Etam. In Smith's Bible Dictionary we find that, in Hebrew, Etam means "A place of ravenous beasts." In this place was a high cliff or lofty rock which led down into a chasm or cleft where Samson went. Going down into this chasm, or place of ravenous beasts, is represented in Physiology by the vital fluid in the spinal cord going down into the seminal vesicles.

ISAIAH 31:7

"For in that day every man shall cast away his idols of silver and his idols of gold, which your own hands have made unto you for a sin."

ISAIAH 28:7-8

"But they also have erred through wine, and through strong drink are out of the way; the priest and the prophet have erred through strong drink, they are swallowed up of wine, they are out of the way through strong drink; they err in vision, they stumble in judgment. For all tables are full of vomit and filthiness, so that there is no place clean."

REVELATION, 22D CHAPTER, VERSES 1, 2

"And he showed me a pure river of water (spinal cord) flowing out of the throne of God (brain), and the Lamb (optic thalamus). "In the midst of the street of it and on either side of the river (both sides) was there the tree of life (pneumogastric nerve), which bare twelve manner of fruits, and yielded *her* fruit *every month* (seed every moon), and the leaves of the tree were (are) for the healing of the nations"—people.

The Indians, in their legend of the "Four trines within the Grand Symbol," call the solar plexus the "seed pod."

"BETWEEN TWO THIEVES"

The words "thief" and "steal" both mean "to operate in secret." Many things may be done in secret that are good, thus: "Give thine alms in secret"; "Let not thy left hand know what thy right hand doeth."

There is a wide difference between the original meaning of words and their common application.

The pineal gland and pituitary body secrete the positive and negative substance along nerves that cross in the medulla, and the seed is crucified between them, and the oil set free ascends to the pineal gland which is made to say: "Lord, remember me when thou cometh into thy kingdom."

Now, as the fluids of the two glands had united and were ascending up the one on the "Right hand of the Father," the central eye, it would naturally say, "This day (now) shalt thou be with me in paradise."

He who spoke and he who replied were one and the same.

"MY YOKE IS EASY AND MY BURDEN IS LIGHT"

YOKE: To cross or bind. Oxen were yoked about the neck.

The nerves from the pituitary and pineal gland unite, and are thus bound together or yoked in the medulla oblongata ("Place of the Skull") and form a Cross.

In regeneration, when the seed crosses in the regular, automatic manner as the plan of salvation designed that it should, the cervical, or neck, functions properly, and the soreness and uneasy feeling so prevalent in all who lead the animal or carnal life, which is "At enmity to God," or the spiritual life, often experience, and complain of, as every physician will testify.

Burden simply means that which is carried, not necessarily something heavy or tiresome.

The seed (any of the characters in Scripture) absorbs and carries the precious oil that flows down the spinal cord—the *"strait,"* up to the cross (yoke), where the "Cup" (cover of minerals) is removed," which frees the precious oil. This illuminating substance then enters the optic and "Giveth light to all that are in the house," or the chamber, the thalamus.

Thus does the redeeming seed truly say, "My burden is light," or illumination.

Paul bears witness thus: "The Christ (oil) in you, the hope of glory"—Glow-ray. Also, "Unless Christ be *raised* then is our preaching vain."

DORMANT BRAIN CELLS

In every brain there are countless dormant brain cells, waiting for the coming of the Air Age, the Bridegroom— or the recognition of the "Christ in the flesh," that will quicken them into activity—*i.e.*, resurrect them.

Everywhere there is evidence of the awakening of dormant brain cells. Spiritual phenomena, multiple personality, mental telepathy and kindred manifestations are explainable upon the hypothesis that dormant brain cells may be made to bloom and thus operate according to new concepts.

We know that there are many millions of dormant brain cells in the cerebrum, especially in the "Most High" portion, the seat of spiritual faculties; or, we may say, the key, which, when touched with the vital fluid set free, "Cast on the waters" and "Lifted up" through the process of physical regeneration, completes the at-one-ment with the Ego, whose indwelling place is the cerebellum. And then the statement, "I and the Father are One," becomes living thunder and flaming light from Sinai, instead of a popular epigram with no vital meaning.

The dormant brain cells may be likened to a flower yet in the bud; but when the substance that is required for their completion reaches them, the modus operandi of the plan of salvation, the buds open, or unfold, and then vibrate at the rate that causes the realization of the New Birth—the "Birth from above."

"He that is born of God will not sin, for *his seed* remaineth in him."

And thus spake Paul: "We shall be changed in the twinkling of an *Eye*"—not *eyes*—but the optic thalamus, the "single," or perfected eye. See chart.

CHILDREN

Child means young, not aged.

"Children of Israel, or "warriors of God." See Smith's Bible Dictionary. There is not now, nor was there ever a geographical, historical land or nation called Israel. The name originated in secret or sacred books which are *not* historical or *outward*, but secret or *inward*.

The seeds that were saved every 29½ days were called the "warriors of God."

"Suffer little children to come unto me, and forbid them not, for of such is the kingdom of heaven."

The seed is small.

"The kingdom of heaven is likened unto a mustard seed."

The seed of all seeds, Jesus, the first seed, asks that other seeds might also be saved, for the seeds, saved and raised to the pineal gland, return to the heaven from which they came.

"Whosoever shall not receive the kingdom of God as a little child, he shall not enter therein."

The lion (animal force) (see Daniel in the lion's den) and the lamb (innocence, or spiritual concept) make at-one-ment (shall lie down together), and "A little child (seed) shall lead them," which means that the seed will carry up one-tenth of the descending fluid in the spinal cord (the great *strait*) to the Father, thus giving tithes to the Lord.

THE PSALMS OF DAVID

David is "Beloved of God"—psalm, "Praise, or hymn."

David is the seed, speaking, praising the source of its being and asking continually that its enemy, the carnal man, be destroyed.

"And David said to Gad, I am in a great *strait*, let me fall into the hands of the Lord and not in the hands of man."

The hands of man refers to the first man, Adam, or ani-mal desire. The strait is the spinal cord—"The strait and narrow way that leads to life eternal."

Gad refers to the tribe of Aries, the ram—the head

ruled by the brain substance—the OR, the Lord, or "Lord God from heaven."

"Jonathan—the praise of Jehovah."

T, or Tav, in Hebrew, means a cross.

H, from Heth, means spiritual perception.

So Jonathan is a symbol of John, the baptizing fluid (oil) that descends from the upper brain that has been lifted by the seed (David), just as John, in the New Testament, was lifted up by Jesus after the baptism.

"HE THAT RULETH HIS OWN SPIRIT (SELF) IS GREATER THAN HE THAT TAKETH A CITY"

"If a man cannot rule his own house, how can he take care of the church of God?"

The Ego resides in and operates from the cerebellum, a house or beth, and is in direct communication with the upper brain, the FATHER, not only by means of the connective tissue partition of ganglia, but also by the wondrous *lever*, the pineal gland, the "Root and the stem of Jesse." Jesse means "a traveler from Bethlehem"—the very same as Jesus, the seed.

The pneumogastric nerve also commences in the medulla oblongata, against the cerebellum, and reaches down to the plexus, branches, in Bethlehem.

The thoughts of the Ego in its home in the cerebellum (called "heart" by the Greeks—"As a man thinketh in his heart so is he") may operate in the lower or Adam man, or in the "Lord God from heaven" realm.

This operation is clearly and startlingly set forth in the ancient, thrice-told parable of the prodigal son, who *thought* it best to take his portion or *substance* and waste, or "eat it," in riotous living. The Ego thus ate of the fruit or bread of the tree of life, so that he did not rule or master himself. The natural sequence to this failure is a deficiency or wasting away of the gray matter of the brain, for the seed that should *lift up* one-tenth (tithe) every 29½ days has been eaten in Egypt and Sodom, "Where our Lord was also crucified." "For he that eateth and drinketh unworthily, eateth and drinketh damnation to himself, not discerning the Lord's body."

[160]

In order to be able to *take* care of the house of God—
"Your body is the temple (house or church) of God,"
one must return a portion to the brain in the "Only way
whereby he may be saved, Jesus Christed and crucified"—
the seed carried up the "Strait and narrow way," and
cross-ified at the "place of the skull."

"AND ENOCH WALKED WITH GOD AND WAS NOT, FOR GOD TOOK HIM"

"Enoch" is Hebrew for initiation, and "Hebrew" means
to Passover. (See "Crossing Jordan," or "Crucifixion.")

"Elijah went up in a chariot of fire." Elijah means
the same as Jesus.

"Elijah's mantle fell on Elisha." Elisha represents the
material for the next seed. "Mantle" means the same as
cover or cup; "Father, remove this cup from me."

"The latchet of whose shoes I am not worthy to un-
loose." Mantle, cup, latchet, and shoes all refer to something that *covers.*

The record states that when Jesus was born he was
"Put in swaddling clothes," or covered. The mineral
salts in the medulla oblongata, through which the pineal
and pituitary fluids flow on the way down the Ida and
Pingala nerves, carry enough of the mineral salts to
form the crust or seed that protects the "Precious Ointment" that is finally released when the seed goes over the
crossed Ida and Pingala, at Golgotha. Hence, "Father
remove this cup (cover) from me."

Again, the "mantle that fell on Elisha" was this same
cup or swaddling cloth that is represented by "As I go
so will I come again." Who? This *same* Jesus, or
"Elisha—Elijah."

"I am the resurrection and the life."

Moses represents the seed, also, found in an ark.

"To Abraham and his seed was the *promise* given,
and to *thy* seed, which is Christ."—Paul.

"Whom do men say that I the Son of man am?

"And they said, Some say that thou are John the Bap-
tist, some Elias, and others, Jeremiah, or one of the
prophets"—*i.e.,* resurrected seeds.

[161]

OM MANI PADME HUM
The Jewel in the Lotus

The lotus flower is the cerebrum, whose convolutions or petals receive all vibrations from without and are transmitted to the mechanism within, there to be translated into terms of the senses. Dew-drops from the boundless sea of the Virgin Mary, the tender mother, glisten on its perfumed petals, while they reflect the golden glory of the spiritual sun.

Countless thousands of these wondrous petals lie tightly closed in the cerebrum of the average person. Sad to relate, there are many, many people in whom the lotus petals have atrophied, died and decayed. Then the asylum or the institution for the feeble minded claims them.

The Optic within the Thalamus is the heart, the fair jewel within the lotus bud. It is the stone the builders rejected.

The spinal cord is the stem of the lotus, a filament from which reaches down into the slime of the asphalt bed.

The Kundalini fire within the sacred plexus is the Bride of the Lot-us, Lot's wife who looked back and became a pillar of salt.

As the dark and slimy bed conceals the quintessence of richness which fertilizes the lotus, and causes it to bud, so the vibrations from the sun above impinge upon this wonderful bud, and the force from above and the force from beneath, meeting in that wondrous heart of the lotus, causes all those beautiful petals to unfold, and lo! its heart lies bare to the universe.

And thus in you and I, when that quintessence of richness is kept within the body—when it is not "wasted in riotous living"—ascends the spinal cord, rising ever higher and higher until at last it reaches the heart of the lotus, the optic thalamus, vivifying it, revealing it, a glowing, scintillating jewel reflecting the light of the Logos Himself and its petals wide open to receive vibrations which translate into the music of the spheres—and once again a lotus has bloomed.

When a human lotus blooms it is said that all nature thrills with gladness and thanksgiving.

THE HUMAN AUTOMOBILE

Man never invented anything. There is no *new* thing.

Within the "Fearfully and wonderfully made" human machine are the vestigial multiple forms conceived in the Infinite Mind, the prototypes of all things; and when the "Spirit in man," the Ego, receives understanding from the "wisdom of the Almighty," it operates on the canvas of life before it, the plane of expression and form, shapes machines, and the factories of a transient commercialism which serve their day like a child's toy, then go into the discard and disappear. One day the coach and four-in-hand, the next day the locomotive. Then man springs upon an automobile and drives it until the axles blaze and the spaces shrivel behind him.

Tomorrow he leaves earth behind and climbs the etheric terraces, peering into the unknown as if searching for the portals of some Celestial City.

The cerebellum is the chauffeur's seat, the pineal gland the lever, the cerebrum the gasoline tank (woe be to him who is out of oil), the solar plexus is the speedometer, and the spinal cord is the passageway from the oil tank.

The individual can run his automobile carefully, wisely, at just the right speed, and with common sense. He can lose control and try to climb a telegraph pole, or go over an embankment. If he or she is a careful driver and looks to the well-being of his machine, he would be careful to have his steering gear in perfect order. If he found his machine had a hole in the gas tank and that the gas was being wasted, he would hasten to have it repaired. Does he ever even think of the oil tank in his own body?

THE HUMAN THERMOMETER

The spinal cord may be likened to a thermometer. The lower part of the vertebrae, the Dead Sea, or the Lake of Asphaltum (Cauda Equina) is the congealed mercury or quicksilver, which may be refined (melted) or raised by heat.

When seeds have been saved so that that body becomes purified, the rate of its vibration has been changed, and at the proper time the wonderful Kundalini, the serpent fire, is released and rises to the top of the cord, going into the head and out through the door of Brahm—which is between the sutures. The mercury thus rises to the 33rd degree and goes over the top, reaching the *shade* or shadow of the Most High; 3 times 3 equals 9; thus 90 degrees in the *shade*.

THE PNEUMOGASTRIC OR VAGUS NERVE OR TREE AND HOLY GHOST

This wonderful nerve is the largest bundle of nerve fibers in the body. It is truly a Tree of Life, and its branches distribute the Holy Breath, essence, or *Ghost*, to lungs and solar plexus.

The breath, speaking from the natural body, is the air breathed into the lungs via the branches of trachea (Greek for rough), commonly termed wind-pipe.

For further information about the breath or *air* see "Turning water into wine." But the office of the pneumogastric *tree* is to conduct and properly distribute the "Holy Ghost," the highly refined substance, a first potency of the breath that "God breathed into man."

When this breath is breathed into the body, about the age of twelve, and unites with the two different potencies of creative "substance" that descends from the "Most High," via the pineal gland, Joseph (or increase), and also through the pituitary gland, Mar-y (pure fluid-water) that have descended the two wonder nerves, extensions of pineal gland and pituitary body, one on each side of the spinal cord, and cross this great Strait between the 12th dorsal vertebra, "in Egypt where our Lord was also crucified"; thence united, they go up to the semilunar ganglio, a *little space* (see chart), thence into the *manger* in Bethlehem. Here the Divine Drama is enacted and "Jesus is conceived of the Holy Ghost"—the whole breath, coming down the pneumogastric tree or nerve.

Pneumo means breath.

Breath in Greek is ghost.

[164]

THE SON OF MAN

"Know ye not that the Son of man hath power *in* earth to forgive sins?"

Who is the Son of man?

"The seed (or word) is the Son of man."

Again, Revelation 19:13—"And his name is called the WORD OF GOD."

REGENERATION

"Ye who have followed (disciple is a follower) me in the regeneration. "Read entire chapter of Matthew 19.

"Sell or exchange what thou hast and give *to the poor.*"

Return one-tenth of the descending substance to the poor pineal gland, the central eye and the upper brain that is slowly but surely wasting away—therefore getting poorer every day. Matt. 19.

How can this poverty be prevented? See Matt. 19. "With *man* (carnal or Adam—of earth, earthy), it is impossible, but with *God all* things are possible."

How shall we come in touch with God and realize our power—*i.e.,* to be perfect, even as our Father in heaven is perfect?

Answer: "When ye pray for anything, *know* that ye have it *now.*"

This means that we recognize that all things exist *now* and that the *upper brain,* the Most High, the great reservoir of "enduring substance" (Paul) will give to the Ego, who resides in the cerebellum (see chart), whatsoever it asks, because the Ego RECOGNIZED the *reality* of the "Secret place of the MOST HIGH."

There are four brains in the human body. The cerebrum, the cerebellum, the medulla oblongata, and the solar plexus.

The Pingala nerve corresponds to the right sympathetic system; the Ida, to the left sympathetic system.

Sushumna passes from the terminus of the spinal cord to the top of the cranium.

"The spino-olivary fasciculus is a small tract, triangular in section, which runs on the surface of the cord and just lateral to the anterior roots of the spinal nerves. This is connected with the Dorsal Spino-cerebellar Fasciculus.

The latter conveys non-sensory sympathetic impulses received from the viscera. In the dorsal part of this nerve is a small strand of fibers called the spinal vestibular tract which rises in the *lumbar-sacral* region of the cord."—Santee. We can easily see the connection between these nerves. The olivary of course has to do with the distribution of the oil and we know that the sacral ganglion is connected with the genitals.

"Fibers of the cerebrum concerned with the *higher* psychic functions of the brain become medullated gradually, year after year, keeping pace with the mental development, and the process of medullation is not completed until late in life."—Kaes.

There is a central canal within the spinal cord. That which is within this canal is of a substance more like steam or gas than anything else.

"AS A MAN THINKETH IN HIS HEART
SO IS HE"

THOUGHT is the creative power in the universe. Universal intelligence, operating as thought, sprang forth, "Spirit-sandalled and shod," at the appointed time and in the appointed place, and Lo! the planet earth, man's sorrowful star, became manifest.

Earth is man's sorrowful star for the reason that only by means of trouble and pain does humanity learn its lessons.

Spirit, manifesting on earth, uses earth as a negative pole, in order that the personality may grow. The mineral, vegetable and animal kingdoms use earth in much the same way. The earth is one plane of manifestation.

How can a man *think* in his *heart?*

The organ that divides blood was called by the ancients "dividing pump"—not heart. The real heart is the cerebellum and was so named by the Greeks and is the seat of thought.

Madame Blavatsky says, in the Secret Doctrine, that the cerebellum contains all, being the seat of intelligence.

The thinker, the individual or "man who never dies," has his home, therefore, in the cerebellum, under the shadow of the Almighty.

Read what the writer of the 91st Psalm has to say about this: "He that dwelleth in the secret place of the Most High shall abide under the shadow of the Almighty."

Secret (secretion, oil or ointment) place of the Most High—is that place where the secretion of oil or ointment is found. In the Bible we see so many references to oil-anointing, secret, secretions, etc.

This plainly shows that the place of the Most High is the cerebrum, that portion of the anatomy of man whence comes the oil or ointment—the precious substance that fructifies the brain of man and causes it to develop; it is that which nourishes the brain.

The abiding place of the Ego *is* "Under the shadow of the Almighty," since the cerebrum extends entirely over and around it.

And again the Psalmist says:

"He will cover thee with his pinions
and under his wings shalt thou take refuge."

The feathery convolutions which are plainly shown in the upper brain may be well compared to the feathers of a bird. The "Voice of the Silence" speaks of the Ego resting "Under the wings of the Great Bird."

The upper brain is composed of highly specialized substance. It is a reservoir of God's creative compounds. It is that God-making material—the Kingdom of Heaven wherein all is found.

"Seek ye first the Kingdom of Heaven and all things shall be added unto you."

"The Kingdom of Heaven is within you."

Heaven means "heaved up"—a high place.

The cerebrum is, then, the kingdom of heaven, for it is within us. By seeking it we draw from it the precious oil or ointment which shall nourish the brain and therefore cause it to grow and expand.

Certain parts of the brain cells are dormant. They are in a certain slow rate of motion or activity, and, therefore, answer to vibrations of their kind.

Let us suppose, for example, that little cell in the brain is composed of spirallae, spirals of nerves, seven sets of which can be seen by the trained occultist.

In a person of low intelligence only three or four of these spirallae will be found to be active, while the man who is already working along the line of regeneration—living the life of self-sacrifice, will show five and six in active operation.

The higher and more lofty the *quality* of the thought, the finer or higher the vibration. Just as the vibration of the ether strikes upon the tympanum of the ear and produces sound—so are the spirallae of the brain cells operated upon by the fingers of the heavenly man, *when* the Kingdom is sought.

Thought, then, is a vibration, and as a man thinks so does he vibrate his brain cells.

How many people really think?

The war has done more to wake people up and set them to thinking than anything else ever could have done. It has started that process in many people—it has forced them to think.

Thought is a particular development of ideas, something entirely apart from the "hit-or-miss," "ramshackle" process which was supposed to be thought.

Let us begin to think; let us *choose* the material from which we shall build our temples—the temple of the "Living God."

The process that the average man calls thought is not consecutive thinking. God hasten the day when people will realize that all that is, has been or will be, is the result of thought.

Thought is both creative and destructive.

Not only are we making our bodies now, but we are making those which we shall wear in the future.

By the future I mean when the individual is reincarnated.

A great thinker has said: "Know this mighty fact, the soul is but the fruitage of thought tinctured and tarnished with the emotions, passions and desires of the flesh."

First, as regards the physical body. Thought selects the food by which the body is nourished. The cells of the body are being constantly destroyed and rebuilt. The purest food possible to obtain will construct a pure body. Vegetables, fruits and grains are of much finer construction than flesh, and hence can vibrate to much higher rates of motion.

Flesh is decaying animal matter and is detrimental to the highest development of man. Much flesh eating thoroughly coarsens the body, and the marks of his calling are stamped on the face of the butcher.

Another example is that of a man who drinks. Alcohol brings about exactly the same result. The body cannot respond to any of the higher vibrations.

Just as surely as the note you strike on the piano must produce a certain tone, just so surely will your body answer to the same rate of vibration around it that vibrates to in itself.

The high cost of flesh food during the war h- been a blessing in disguise, for it was the only mea- whereby people could be brought to realize that th- could still *live* if they never ate meat. Then, after a tin- they will begin to realize that they can enjoy much bett- health without it.

If you wished to do a fine, delicate piece of work, y- would not use coarse or unwieldy instruments in doing

Just as true is it that the vehicle of the spirit—Sol- mon's Temple—must be delicately and finely constructe-

The body must be kept scrupulously clean and be giv- sufficient exercise.

If your body is not satisfactory to you, it is becau- you have indulged in thoughts that have marred its co- struction.

It is never too late to do *something* toward the reco- struction and regeneration of the body.

Start *NOW*.

The physical man is made up of twelve divisions, *i. e* bone man, muscular man, nerve man, etc. These are a- constructed with a certain cell salt or mineral as a ba- for each man or division of the body, see "Relation of tl- Mineral Salts of the Blood to the Signs of the Zodiac

Each cell of the body is a *living*, throbbing intelligenc- Each cell actually reaches out and grasps from out tl- water of life—that living stream of blood that is the li- of the body—just the material it needs in its constructio-

"The quality of the force called into action in any kin- dom determines the quality of the offspring."

You are directly responsible for each thought th- occupies your brain.

The soul is the thought man and the emotional ma- that occupies the physical bodies resembles it in form an- feature. We do not here refer to the Spiritual Ego.

If, then, our thoughts build our bodies, what though- are the cell lives of the body filled with? We must natu- ally see that they are, in vast numbers, filled wit- thoughts of fear, strife and blood. Fears of microbe-disease, poverty, the neighbors, the weather, the night air, the dark, burglars, etc., etc.

Eternal strife for wealth, position and power, for material benefits. Benefits, so-called.

All this brings about war—the cell life gorged with blood, calling for the blood of its brothers.

Is not the cause of the war clear?

Do not thoughts pollute the very air? Is it not true that our thoughts affect those around us? What about the cells that we throw off from our bodies every minute —cells that we have built and that are impregnated with our thoughts?

What is the matter with the people in the world? For there is nothing the matter with the world itself.

Each cell, then, that we throw off from our bodies, hour by hour and day by day, bears the stamp of our thoughts upon it. These go to make up the record of our lives, which those whose eyes are opened can read. In occultism this is called the Akashic record.

Then each man is the recording angel.

"Like attracts like." Birds of a feather flock together." These are trite sayings.

We see, then, that the cellular construction and fineness of the tissues of the physical man is determined by the character of the thoughts we store away in them.

The prodigal son wasted his substance in riotous living. His thoughts were turned toward the indulgence of the lower passions, like the rich young man who went away sorrowful because he had many possessions. Therefore the precious substance, the oil or ointment, the elixir of life, was sold for a mess of pottage. The seed, Jesus, or Christ, was not saved. If his thoughts had been pure and clean, the seed would have reached the cerebellum and would have increased in power a thousand fold. They then would have become the anointed of the Lord— would have received the oil or oinment. The prodigal would then have become the son "in whom the Father was well pleased."

When the thoughts of the disciple are purified from every undesirable thought—then he becomes the son of the Master for his thought flows like a river through the consciousness of his Lord.

His body has become transfigured, for each seed has become crucified and Christed. Each cell of his body has thrown off all its impurities and has become *white* in the blood of the lamb, for the blood of the lamb is as a crystal stream.

The process of regeneration causes the white corpuscles of the blood to overcome the preponderance of red, or Mars corpuscles.

Therefore the flesh becomes transparent—and he manifests more and more of the Father—he is no longer man—but has become a God.

Paul says: "Now, then, are we the sons of God."

"All things I have done ye can do, and greater."

As we go on living the regenerative life, the time comes when we no longer respond to any law within the physical realm, for all physical matter has been cast off from the body. "It is sown a material and is *raised* (because the seed has been raised—the rate of vibration has been raised) a *spiritual* body, and the Kingdom of Heaven has been attained.

"HE THAT OVERCOMETH"

The above sentence occurs nine times in Revelation.

To overcome a vice or habit means *to cease to do* it. In the Scriptures overcome is used to symbol the triumph of the Ego over sex or animal desire. It means the conquering of the carnal mind.

REVELATION 2, 7—"He that hath an ear, let him hear what the Spirit saith unto the churches; To him that overcometh will I give to eat of the tree of life, which is in the midst of the paradise of God."

REVELATION 2, 11—"He that hath an ear, let him hear what the Spirit saith unto the churches; He that overcometh shall not be hurt of the second death."

REVELATION 2, 17—"He that hath an ear, let him hear what the Spirit saith unto the churches; To him that overcometh will I give to eat of the hidden manna, and I will give him a white stone, and in the stone a new name written, which no man knoweth saving he that receiveth it."

REVELATION 2, 26, 27—"And he that overcometh, and keepeth my works unto the end, to him will I give power over the nations." "And he shall rule them with a rod of iron; as the vessels of a potter shall they be broken to shivers; even as I received of my Father. And I will give him the morning star."

REVELATION 3, 5—"He that overcometh, the same shall be clothed in white raiment; and I will not blot out his name out of the book of life, but I will confess his name before my Father, and before his angels."

REVELATION 3, 12—"Him that overcometh will I make a pillar in the temple of my God, and he shall go no more out: and I will write upon him the name of my God, and the name of the city of my God, which is new Jerusalem, which cometh down out of heaven from my God: and I will write upon him my new name."

REVELATION 3, 21—"To him that overcometh will I grant to sit with me in my throne, even as I also overcame, and am set down with my Father in his throne."

REVELATION 21, 7—"He that overcometh shall inherit all things; and I will be his God, and he shall be my son."

EXTRACT FROM "DISCOURSES FROM THE SPIRIT-WORLD

By Rev. R. P. Wilson; Dictated by Stephen Olin
(Published in 1853)

I T IS thought that Stephen Olin was First President of Wesleyan University.

"The inhabitants of the earth may look forward with joyful assurance that the time is approaching when heaven shall be manifest on earth in the glorious harmonies that will everywhere greet the eye and cheer the heart. *As certain as the revolutions of time move forward,* SO SURELY WILL THE DIVINE GLORY BE VISIBLY DISPLAYED AND ALL NATIONS SHALL BEHOLD AND ENJOY THE BLESSEDNESS OF CELESTIAL *ILLUMINATION.* Such being the future and happy result that awaits the earth and its inhabitants, how important, fellow mortal, is *your duty* to hasten on the grand consummation. Arise from your inactivity and dullness and *move forward* in obedience to the laws of your being. Let no excuse prevent the utmost development of your whole nature. Exercise all the powers of your mind and body with reference to the harmonial unfolding of yourself. Do what you can to assist others in the great work of spiritual and physical development. Learn from the volume of inspiration in the universe without, and let your spirit look within for still higher manifestations and *more refined* enjoyments.

CONSUMMATION
1927

THE revolutionary planet Uranus will have completed his seven years' journey through Pisces, and
entered the sign Aries, representing the upper brain,
in January, 1927.

The stars in their course
Are nearing the dawn of peace.
The purpling mountain-tops
Of human love appear.
Look! Listen!
Above the battle's din you may hear
The anthem of "Peace on earth."
Good will to men is in the air.
Out from the curling mists of the Pacific Sea
That twist and twine
Like things alive;
From the glory of the upclimbing clouds
Of the morning, that spill their jewels
On the grass and flowers;
In the liquid notes of the shuttle-throated mocking bird
That pours its rippling prayers
Into the ears of Deity;
From the clean-trunked eucalypti,
From orange blossoms and pendant pepper bough;
From the sweet-faced little children;
From the hearts of earnest men;
From the souls of women—mothers;
From the planetary angles
And rising constellations;
From the heavenly hosts that
"Declare the glory of God";
From the inner sanctuary of cosmic law—
We may hear the song of Peace.
Peace comes!
Reach forth thy hands, brothers, sisters,
Welcome thy Savior—Peace.

Offend her not!
Bow to the radiant queen!
We are so weary—
Yea, sick unto death—of war.
Our Healer comes—
The Great Physician.
Let all rejoice and be glad.
Let us join the song, Peace unto Thee!

From the Seven Sacred Centers of regenerate human bodies; from the Secret Places of the Most High, where immortal Egos sit enthroned in the wondrous brain of man—the new Jerusalem—is heard the Divine Anthem. The music of the Spheres, out and out in realms of Cosmic Law, now becomes audible, and choruses with the redeemed and glorified earth.

Flowers bloom fresh in her footsteps;
The folds of her white garments are like "trailing clouds of glory."
The co-operative commonwealth of humanity looms behind her.
The bugles all sing truce along the iron front of war.
Ironclads rust.
Airships climb and climb into the ether,
As if seeking the portals of the Celestial City.
The trenches are covered with grass.
Vines clamber over arsenals,
Flowers bloom on deserted forts.
Soldiers become men at home, field, shop, firesides,
Women love and children play.
"The ransomed of the Lord return
And come to Zion—
With everlasting joy upon their heads."
And all over and about
The air is full of the scent of flowers,
And the trickling fall of fountains,
And free men and women have started on the Great Adventure
To find God.

  * * * * * * * *

"And I saw a New Heaven and a New Earth,"
The old has passed away and the sun of righteousness arises with Healing in its beams.

THE END

CPSIA information can be obtained
at www.ICGtesting.com
Printed in the USA
LVHW060043240123
737807LV00004B/29

9 781169 276277